The Children *of* Fatima

Student Workbook

Copyright © 2016 TAN Books

All rights reserved. No part of this book may be reproduced or transmitted in any form or by any means, electronic or mechanical, including photocopying, recording, or by any information storage or retrieval system, without permission in writing from the publisher, except that brief selections may be quoted or copied for non-profit use without permission.

Cataloging-in-Publication data on file with the Library of Congress.

Illustrations by Gedge Harmon

ISBN: 978-1-5051-0711-1

Published in the United States by
TAN Books
PO Box 269
Gastonia, NC 28053
www.TANBooks.com

Printed and bound in the United States of America

The Children of Fatima

Student Workbook

a comprehensive companion to the book by
Mary Fabyan Windeatt

CHAPTER 1: The Angel of Peace

Key Terms

These are important people, places, and things you should remember from this chapter.

Fatima   A village in Portugal where Jacinta, Francisco, and Lucia lived.

Jacinta   Sister to Francisco and cousin to Lucia.

Francisco   Brother to Jacinta and cousin to Lucia.

Lucia   Cousin to Jacinta and Francisco.

Angel of Peace   The angel who appeared to the children and revealed his name as the Guardian Angel of Portugal.

Vocabulary

*Read the sentences below and note the use of the word in **bold**. Write a definition or synonym for this word by considering its context.*

1. The next moment he was gone, leaving the children more **awestruck** than they had ever been in their lives.

2. Offer it to God as an act of **reparation** for the sins by which He is offended and as a petition for the conversion of sinners.

3. Above all, accept and bear with **submission** the suffering that the Lord will send you.

4. The children joined in this **sublime** prayer to the Holy Trinity as best they could.

4 | *The Children of Fatima*   Mary Fabyan Windeatt

The Angel of Peace

CHAPTER 1

Comprehension Questions

To better understand this chapter, ask yourself these questions and write down your answers using complete sentences.

1. What did Jacinta, Francisco, and Lucia often do before dawn?
   ....
   ....
   ....

2. What was different about the way the three children typically said the Rosary?
   ....
   ....
   ....

3. What strange sight did the children see in the cave on that first day?
   ....
   ....
   ....

4. The Angel of Peace asked the children to pray a specific prayer. What were the intentions of this prayer?
   ....
   ....
   ....

5. What other name did the Angel give to the children on his second visit? How did he say the children could convert sinners?
   ....
   ....
   ....

The Children of Fatima Mary Fabyan Windeatt

CHAPTER 2

Another Visitor

Key Terms

These are important people, places, and things you should remember from this chapter.

Cova da Iria A large hollow about a mile from the homes of the children in Fatima.

Maria das Neves A young girl who had died recently and was in heaven, according to the beautiful lady from heaven.

Amelia A young girl who had died recently and would be in purgatory until the end of the world, according to the beautiful lady from heaven.

Vocabulary

Read the sentences below and note the use of the word in **bold**. *Write a definition or synonym for this word by considering its context.*

1. On May 13, 1917, slightly more than a year after the Angel's first visit, the three children were **pasturing** their flocks as usual.

2. She wore a long white dress, and the white mantle over her head and shoulders was edged in **burnished** gold.

3. Francisco and Jacinta had been silent during the entire length of the **apparition**—ten minutes or so.

4. We must all say the Rosary, very **devoutly**, every day.

5. Their mother's amazement knew no **bounds**.

The Children of Fatima Mary Fabyan Windeatt

Another Visitor

CHAPTER 2

Comprehension Questions

To better understand this chapter, ask yourself these questions and write down your answers using complete sentences.

1. Why was Francisco puzzled about the Angel's request for them to offer all their suffering for the conversion of sinners?

   ....
   ....
   ....

2. Where were the children when they thought they were seeing extraordinary lightning? What were they actually seeing?

   ....
   ....
   ....

3. How did the beautiful lady answer Lucia's questions about where she came from and what she wanted?

   ....
   ....
   ....

4. What did the Lady say about the two girls, Maria das Neves and Amelia, who had died recently?

   ....
   ....
   ....

5. What was unique about the way each child perceived the visit from the beautiful lady?

   ....
   ....
   ....

The Children of Fatima Mary Fabyan Windeatt

CHAPTER 3

The Lady Comes Again

Key Terms

These are important people, places, and things you should remember from this chapter.

Father Marques Ferreira A parish priest to the families of the children.

Porto-de-Mos A neighboring village to Fatima.

Feast of St. Anthony A great feast day celebrated by those in Portugal for the saint who had died in Padua but still belonged to Portugal.

Lisbon The capital of Portugal where St. Anthony had been born.

Vocabulary

*Read the sentences below and note the use of the word in **bold**. Write a definition or synonym for this word by considering its context.*

1. Lucia's mother lost no time in punishing her daughter for what she considered to be a **willful** foolishness.

2. Suddenly Lucia's mother reached a **grim** decision: this ten-year-old daughter was more stubborn than she had thought.

3. Early the next morning, the road leading from Fatima to Porto-de-Mos was dotted with **lumbering** farm wagons.

4. The little shepherds paid **scant** attention to the grown-ups who had come to watch them.

8 | *The Children of Fatima* Mary Fabyan Windeatt

The Lady Comes Again

CHAPTER 3

Comprehension Questions

To better understand this chapter, ask yourself these questions and write down your answers using complete sentences.

1. Who was angry upon finding out about the children's vision and why?
   ....
   ....
   ....

2. To whom did Lucia's mother bring her to talk about the visions?
   ....
   ....
   ....

3. What did Father Ferreira say to the children's mothers?
   ....
   ....
   ....

4. Who attended the Lady's second visit at the Cova?
   ....
   ....
   ....

5. What prayer did the Lady ask the children to recite after the *Gloria* of each mystery of the Rosary?
   ....
   ....
   ....

The Children of Fatima   Mary Fabyan Windeatt

CHAPTER 4 — The Message

Key Terms

These are important people, places, and things you should remember from this chapter.

Immaculate Heart The Lady told them this was her heart: the heart of the Blessed Virgin.

Five First Saturdays An Act of Reparation to the Immaculate Heart, where a person goes to Confession and receives communion on these days, as well as says the Rosary and spends fifteen minutes meditating on the mysteries of the Rosary.

Aljustrel A town just outside of Fatima in Portugal.

Vocabulary

*Read the sentences below and note the use of the word in **bold**. Write a definition or synonym for this word by considering its context.*

1. The Lady sensed Lucia's **bewilderment**.

2. For a moment the three children stared **forlornly** after her.

3. Lucia pointed **resolutely** to the small holm oak.

4. But suddenly the air was filled with the sound of **babbling** tongues.

The Message

CHAPTER 4

Comprehension Questions

To better understand this chapter, ask yourself these questions and write down your answers using complete sentences.

1. When the Lady stretched out her hands, what did all three children experience?
   ....
   ....
   ....

2. The Lady offered assistance to people at the hour of their death. But what did she say people had to do to receive this assistance?
   ....
   ....
   ....

3. Who did the children forget about after the Lady left them because they were so distracted by their discussion of her visit?
   ....
   ....
   ....

4. Lucia told the people a little bit about the Lady's visit. What was their reaction?
   ....
   ....
   ....

5. What did the children do when people began to doubt their vision and call them actors?
   ....
   ....
   ....

CHAPTER 4: The Message

Activity

The following is an optional activity to expand your knowledge on the holm oak tree where the Lady of Fatima appeared many times to the children of Fatima.

The Lady appeared atop a holm oak tree. Do some research about the holm oak tree and write down at least three characteristics of this tree. Draw a picture of the tree with its leaves, flowers, or acorns.

1. ....
   ....
   ....

2. ....
   ....
   ....

3. ....
   ....
   ....

CHAPTER 4: The Message

Draw the holm oak tree with its leaves, flowers, and acorns.

CHAPTER 5 — A New Life

Key Terms

These are important people, places, and things you should remember from this chapter.

First World War Took place from 1914 to 1918 and was happening during the Lady's visits to the children.

Pius XI Was to become a pope and reign from 1922 to 1939.

Russia The Lady told the children that this country would be converted and would have peace if people followed her request.

Vocabulary

*Read the sentences below and note the use of the word in **bold**. Write a definition or synonym for this word by considering its context.*

1. "What do you want of us?" asked Lucia eagerly, **heedless** of the fact that this time five thousand people were watching her every movement.

2. How **reverently** the children listened to the sweet and sorrowful voice.

3. "In Portugal, the **dogma** of the Faith will always be preserved . . ."

4. The child's four sisters and brother had made her understand that she was bringing **disgrace** on the family by her actions.

5. Then the faithful will become **martyrs**; the Holy Father will have much to suffer, various nations will be destroyed.

A New Life

CHAPTER 5

Comprehension Questions

To better understand this chapter, ask yourself these questions and write down your answers using complete sentences.

1. How many people were on hand for the Lady's third appearance in July?

   ....
   ....
   ....

2. When Lucia asked the Lady for her identity, how did she respond?

   ....
   ....
   ....

3. What did the Lady give the children a vision of during this visit? How many secrets did she tell them?

   ....
   ....
   ....

4. How did Lucia's family treat her after this third visit?

   ....
   ....
   ....

5. How did the children enter a "new life" after the Lady's third visit when she told them the secrets?

   ....
   ....
   ....

The Children of Fatima   Mary Fabyan Windeatt

CHAPTER 5 — A New Life

Activity

The following is an optional activity used to help your comprehension of the text. Answer the questions and locate the answers in the Word Search.

1. A person who dies for his or her faith.

2. The child who spoke to the Lady.

3. The child who could see and hear the Lady but did not speak to her.

4. The child who could see the Lady but not hear her.

5. The place where damned souls go for eternity.

6. The Lady told Lucia that all three children would go to _____ one day.

7. During her third visit, the Lady told the children three _____.

8. One of the secrets the Lady told the children was about the end of the _____, which was happening during this time.

9. The children made many small _____ as penance for sinners.

10. The children had the visions of the Lady at the _____.

11. The Lady told them her heart was the _____ Heart.

12. The children lived in a town called _____.

13. The town from #12 was in what country?

The Children of Fatima Mary Fabyan Windeatt

A New Life

CHAPTER 5

```
K S S C C G I X P O S K E P K
C Z T Z O Z D O O H E T M E Z
S U R E O V R D N F A T I M A
E P Y R R T A E D L E P W H Q
C R T O U C V D U Q Z H O E T
I B R G E A E C A W A L R L O
F G A P E U A S Q I Y W L L L
I L M H O M U W V L R H D D Y
R O S Q M K K T D Q A A W I N
C I Q I A T N I C A J T A U C
A F R A N C I S C O L P R Y Z
S O P C I J X K Y T B U I O G
T Q K Q D G Q C X Y R Q C F L
G Y J T D G D T M L A Z M I R
X T Y Z B N M G B J O K M V A
```

Note: *Some words may appear backward.*

The Children of Fatima   Mary Fabyan Windeatt | **17**

Name _____ Date _____ Score _____

Vocabulary

Complete the crossword puzzle using the definitions and synonyms below as clues. All answers will come from the vocabulary sections covered so far. Look back over these sections if you need assistance completing the puzzle. This should be the only part of the quiz where you can view your notes from previous sections.

1.5 points each (19.5 points)

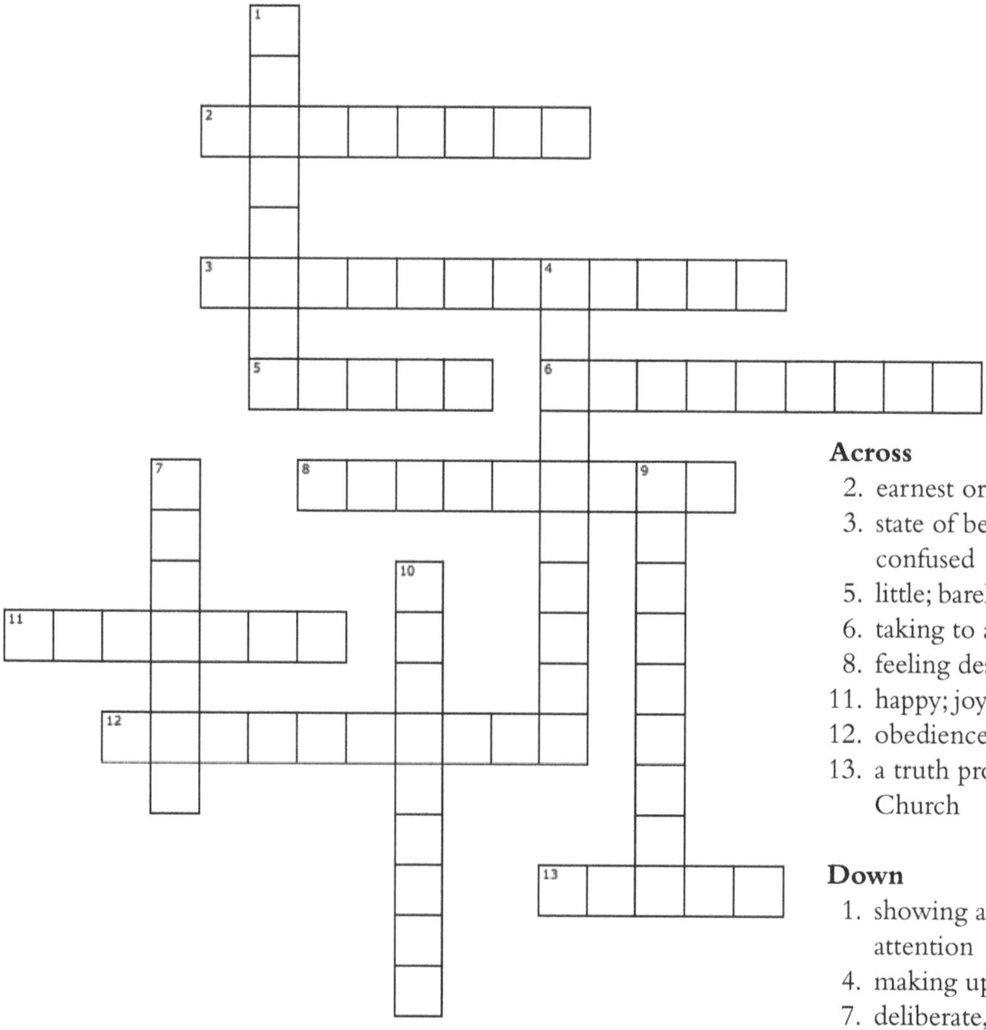

Across

2. earnest or sincere
3. state of being puzzled or confused
5. little; barely
6. taking to a grazing area
8. feeling deserted or sad
11. happy; joyful
12. obedience; acceptance
13. a truth proclaimed by the Church

Down

1. showing a lack of care or attention
4. making up for sin
7. deliberate, voluntary, or intentional
9. heavy and moving clumsily
10. filled with reverence and wonder
12. Heavy and moving clumsily

Chapters 1–5

QUIZ 1

Key Terms

Match the correct term to its definition.

2 points each (36 points)

_____ A village in Portugal where the children lived.

_____ Sister to Francisco and cousin to Lucia.

_____ Brother to Jacinta and cousin to Lucia.

_____ Cousin to Jacinta and Francisco.

_____ The angel who appeared to the children who revealed his name as the Guardian Angel of Portugal.

_____ A large hollow about a mile from the homes of the children in Fatima.

_____ A young girl who had died recently and was in heaven, according to the beautiful lady from heaven.

_____ A young girl who had died recently and would be in purgatory until the end of the world.

_____ A parish priest to the families of the children.

_____ A neighboring village to Fatima.

_____ A great feast day celebrated by those in Portugal for the saint who had died in Padua but still belonged to Portugal.

_____ The capital of Portugal. St. Anthony was born here.

_____ The Lady told them this was her heart; the heart of the Blessed Virgin.

_____ An Act of Reparation to the Immaculate Heart, where you go to Confession, receive Communion on these days, and say the Rosary and spend fifteen minutes meditating on the mysteries of the Rosary.

_____ A town just outside of Fatima in Portugal.

_____ Took place from 1914 to 1918 and was happening during the Lady's visits to the children.

_____ Was to become a pope and reign from 1922 to 1939.

_____ The Lady told the children that this country would be converted and would have peace if people followed her request.

A. Aljustrel
B. Amelia
C. Angel of Peace
D. Cova da Iria
E. Father Marques Ferreira
F. Fatima
G. Feast of St. Anthony
H. First World War
I. Five First Saturdays
J. Francisco
K. Immaculate Heart
L. Jacinta
M. Lisbon
N. Lucia
O. Maria das Neves
P. Pius XI
Q. Porto-de-Mos
R. Russia

Chapters 1–5

Multiple Choice

Choose the correct response and circle the answer.

3 points each (30 points)

1. What did the children experience when, during her second visit, the Lady stretched out her hands?
    a. love
    b. joy
    c. warmth
    d. all of the above

2. Who did the children first see at Cova da Iria?
    a. Angel of Peace
    b. Jesus
    c. a beautiful lady
    d. Holy Spirit

3. What were the children actually seeing when they thought they were seeing lightning?
    a. a great storm
    b. a guardian angel
    c. a beautiful lady
    d. a tornado

4. What did the Lady give the children a vision of during her third visit?
    a. Heaven
    b. the Holy Family
    c. Russia
    d. Hell

5. To whom did Lucia's mother bring her to talk about the visions?
    a. her father
    b. the parish priest
    c. a psychologist
    d. the pope

6. Who could speak to the beautiful lady?
    a. Jacinta
    b. Francisco
    c. no one
    d. Lucia

7. What job did Jacinta, Francisco, and Lucia do every morning for their families?
    a. milk the cows
    b. tend the sheep
    c. wash the dishes
    d. collect the eggs

8. How many people were at the Lady's second visit to the Cova along with the children?
    a. 70
    b. 10
    c. 700
    d. 1,000

20 | *The Children of Fatima* Mary Fabyan Windeatt

Chapters 1–5

QUIZ 1

9. What day of the week did the Lady tell the children people should go to Confession, Communion, say the Rosary, and reflect on the mysteries of the Rosary?

   a. Sunday
   b. Friday
   c. Saturday
   d. Wednesday

10. How many people were in attendance for the Lady's third visit to the Cova?

    a. 5,000
    b. 50
    c. 10,000
    d. 0

Narration Exercise

The remaining 14.5 points of the quiz will come from this narration exercise. Answer the question below in 2–5 complete sentences.

When the Lady visited the third time, she gave the children a vision of something. What was it? How many secrets did she give the children during this visit, and what were these secrets?

The Children of Fatima   Mary Fabyan Windeatt | **21**

An Unexpected Journey

Key Terms

These are important people, places, and things you should remember from this chapter.

Communism A system of government in which a single party controls state-owned means of production with the aim of establishing a stateless society.

Atheist A person who believes that God does not exist.

Ourem The nearest town of any size to Fatima.

Mayor of Ourem A man who tried to deviously stop the children from visiting Cova da Iria and force them to admit they were lying.

Antonio dos Santos The father of Lucia.

Manuel Marto The father of Jacinta and Francisco.

Vocabulary

*Read the sentences below and note the use of the word in **bold**. Write a definition or synonym for this word by considering its context.*

1. With a little **coaxing**, they could be made to confess that the whole affair was a fraud.

2. The mayor's **crafty** eyes lit up.

3. So the message was **dispatched** to Fatima.

4. "Thousands of stupid pilgrims will go into **hysterics**."

5. The car had shot past the church and now was slowing down before an **imposing** and familiar building.

An Unexpected Journey

CHAPTER 6

Comprehension Questions

To better understand this chapter, ask yourself these questions and write down your answers using complete sentences.

1. Which important man was infuriated when he found out about the children's visions?
   ....
   ....
   ....

2. Who did the mayor summon first about the visits? Who actually came?
   ....
   ....
   ....

3. Did the mayor's threats work on Lucia? What did he decide to do after she left?
   ....
   ....
   ....

4. Where did the mayor tell the children he would be taking them?
   ....
   ....
   ....

5. Where did the mayor actually take the children?
   ....
   ....
   ....

The Children of Fatima Mary Fabyan Windeatt

CHAPTER 7 | The Test

Key Terms

These are important people, places, and things you should remember from this chapter.

The mayor's wife   A woman who was ashamed of her husband's actions and treated the children with care.

Vocabulary

*Read the sentences below and note the use of the word in **bold**. Write a definition or synonym for this word by considering its context.*

1. The three stared at each other in **dismay**.

2. Suddenly they felt as though a clean breeze had swept through their **dismal** quarters.

3. Childish trebles telling the praises of the Blessed Virgin, accompanied by a **faltering** chorus of deep-pitched voices.

4. Now he assured them **gloatingly** they did not have a single friend left.

5. Suddenly Lucia could bear the **strain** no longer and stretched forth her arms toward Heaven.

The Test — CHAPTER 7

Comprehension Questions

To better understand this chapter, ask yourself these questions and write down your answers using complete sentences.

1. Where did the mayor bring the children? Who else was there?
   ....
   ....
   ....

2. How did the children respond to the prisoners accusing them of pickpocketing?
   ....
   ....
   ....

3. What did Jacinta ask of one of the prisoners? What was she planning to do?
   ....
   ....
   ....

4. How did the prisoners react to the three children saying the Rosary in their cell?
   ....
   ....
   ....

5. Where did the mayor take the children when he discovered that prison did not seem to scare them?
   ....
   ....
   ....

The Children of Fatima   Mary Fabyan Windeatt

CHAPTER 8

The Fourth Visit

Key Terms

These are important people, places, and things you should remember from this chapter.

Maria Rosa dos Santos The mother of Lucia.

Olimpia Marto The mother of Jacinta and Francisco.

Valinhos A village some distance from the children's home.

Vocabulary

Read the sentences below and note the use of the word in **bold**. *Write a definition or synonym for this word by considering its context.*

1. The children began to **readjust** themselves to the everyday world.

2. Why, I thought as any **sensible** creature would think.

3. But then something truly extraordinary happened, and the whole **atmosphere** had changed.

4. In a moment, she had disappeared into thin air, leaving the young shepherds gazing after her with **rapt** faces.

The Fourth Visit

CHAPTER 8

Comprehension Questions

To better understand this chapter, ask yourself these questions and write down your answers using complete sentences.

1. What did Lucia discover when the mayor brought her to the kitchen to be boiled?
   ....
   ....
   ....

2. What did Lucia's mother believe about the children's captivity?
   ....
   ....
   ....

3. How many people were at the Cova on August 13?
   ....
   ....
   ....

4. What did the people at the Cova see on that day?
   ....
   ....
   ....

5. What came as a surprise the day after the children were released from the mayor?
   ....
   ....
   ....

The Children of Fatima Mary Fabyan Windeatt

CHAPTER 9

New Crowds in the Cova

Key Terms

These are important people, places, and things you should remember from this chapter.

Saint Joseph   The husband of Mary and foster father of Jesus who was to accompany the Lady to the Cova in October.

Newspaperman   A man who tried to convince the people everything the children did was a trick for publicity.

Vocabulary

Read the sentences below and note the use of the word in **bold**. *Write a definition or synonym for this word by considering its context.*

1. She did admit that the branch Lucia had brought home gave forth a wonderfully sweet **fragrance.**

2. She was about to **manifest** herself to these three children of Fatima!

3. "People often arrange affairs like this to get free **publicity**."

4. He continued to declare that the three little shepherds were **conspirators** in a scheme to make money for the parish church.

5. "After all, we should be very **prudent** in this whole matter of the Lady and her visits."

The Children of Fatima   Mary Fabyan Windeatt

New Crowds in the Cova | CHAPTER 9

Comprehension Questions

To better understand this chapter, ask yourself these questions and write down your answers using complete sentences.

1. What did devout men and women do leading up to the Lady's September visit? How did others who were not so devout prepare?

   ....
   ....
   ....

2. What did Lucia say as the children approached the holm oak tree?

   ....
   ....
   ....

3. What did the crowd of people see during the Lady's visit?

   ....
   ....
   ....

4. What did the Lady tell the children about her October visit?

   ....
   ....
   ....

5. What happened when the Lady departed the Cova?

   ....
   ....
   ....

The Children of Fatima   Mary Fabyan Windeatt

New Crowds in the Cova

Activity

The following is an optional activity used to help your comprehension of the text. Answer the questions and locate the answers in the Word Search.

1. The Lady visited _____ when the children missed the August visit due to the mayor.

2. Lucia's mother's name is _____ _____ dos Santos.

3. The Lady said she would bring Saint _____ with her in October.

4. The Lady told the children she would bring the Child_____ along with Saint Joseph.

5. A _____ insisted the children were acting to get free publicity.

6. The parish priest, Father _____, had never come to the Cova during the Lady's visits.

7. Father Ferreira believed the _____ _____ had chosen the children to do a special work for souls.

8. The _____ of Ourem kidnapped the children to try to scare them into admitting the visits were a lie.

9. The father of Jacinta and Francisco, named _____ Marto.

10. The father of Lucia, named _____ dos Santos.

11. The mayor drove the children from Fatima to _____ to keep them away from the Cova.

12. The mother of Francisco and Jacinta, named _____ Marto.

New Crowds in the Cova

CHAPTER 9

```
V A N T O N I O Z Y J P B S T
G L S L L T K R K O E L U O M
M R O O D X I O S M E W O H E
A K U V R E J E G S U K G N R
N A L Y R A P G S U S E J I U
U N O R R H I E R E C I O L O
E Z E L M O D R D J A H D A G
L F C G I V Y A A N L Q S V G
L N W S I M K A X M F N U M N
U P I R H P P Z M C N Q D G O
E L G Q Q K W I L C P Q D J E
B I N A M R E P A P S W E N U
N X I R U J L S P K M S T B Q
H G A I L F Y L X P R T S I I
O E P D U X K S A K O R C M O
```

Note: *Some words may appear backward.*

The Children of Fatima Mary Fabyan Windeatt | **31**

The Great Miracle

Key Terms

These are important people, places, and things you should remember from this chapter.

Holy Family   The Child Jesus with His mother, the Blessed Virgin, and foster father, Saint Joseph.

Lady of Sorrows   A name for the Blessed Virgin. She revealed herself to Lucia in this form on October 13.

Our Lady of Mount Carmel   A name for the Blessed Virgin. She revealed herself to Lucia in a brown habit holding the scapular of Mount Carmel.

Vocabulary

Read the sentences below and note the use of the word in **bold**. *Write a definition or synonym for this word by considering its context.*

1. There in the cold downpour, seventy thousand voices were now raised in honest **supplication**.

2. The rain was over and the sun, hidden for hours by the **ominous** clouds, was now shining in a clear blue sky!

3. Seventy thousand people stood **spellbound**.

4. Their faces were blank with astonishment at this spectacle of a silver sun revolving in a **myriad** of colored rays.

5. The Child Jesus was about a year old, and He was **nestling** in Saint Joseph's arms.

The Great Miracle

Comprehension Questions

To better understand this chapter, ask yourself these questions and write down your answers using complete sentences.

1. Why was Lucia's mother worried about being disgraced on the morning of October 13?

   ....
   ....
   ....

2. What is the first question Lucia asked upon the Lady's arrival? How was it answered?

   ....
   ....
   ....

3. What happened when Our Lady opened her hands and made her own light reflect on the sun?

   ....
   ....
   ....

4. How did the crowd react to the miracle of the sun?

   ....
   ....
   ....

5. What other miracle was experienced by the entire crowd during Our Lady's visit?

   ....
   ....
   ....

The Children of Fatima   Mary Fabyan Windeatt

Vocabulary

Complete the crossword puzzle using the definitions and synonyms below as clues. All answers will come from the vocabulary sections covered so far. Look back over these sections if you need assistance completing the puzzle. This should be the only part of the quiz where you can view your notes from previous sections.

2 points each (28 points)

Across
4. humble petition
6. cunning, sly, tricky
10. uncontrolled emotional outbursts
12. entranced, fascinated
13. immense number

Down
1. a pleasant, sweet smell
2. spreading of information
3. sent off
5. moving or speaking unsteadily
7. threatening
8. very impressive
9. gloomy
11. gentle persuasion or convincing

Chapters 6–10

QUIZ 2

Key Terms

Match the correct term to its definition.

2 points each (30 points)

_____ A system of government in which a single party controls state-owned means of production with the aim of establishing a stateless society.

_____ A person who believes that God does not exist.

_____ The nearest town of any size to Fatima.

_____ A man who tried to deviously stop the children from visiting Cova da Iria and force them to admit they were lying.

_____ The father of Lucia.

_____ The father of Jacinta and Francisco.

_____ A woman who was ashamed of her husband's actions and treated the children with care.

_____ The mother of Lucia.

_____ The mother of Jacinta and Francisco.

_____ A village some distance from the children's home.

_____ The husband of Mary and foster father of Jesus who was to accompany the Lady to the Cova in October.

_____ A man who tried to convince the people everything the children did was a trick for publicity.

_____ The Child Jesus with His mother, the Blessed Virgin, and foster father, Saint Joseph.

_____ A name for the Blessed Virgin. She revealed herself to Lucia in this form on October 13.

_____ A name for the Blessed Virgin. She revealed herself to Lucia in a brown habit holding the scapular of Mount Carmel.

A. Antonio dos Santos
B. Atheist
C. Communism
D. Holy Family
E. Lady of Sorrows
F. Manuel Marto
G. Maria Rosa dos Santos
H. Mayor of Ourem
I. Newspaperman
J. Olimpia Marto
K. Our Lady of Mount Carmel
L. Ourem
M. Saint Joseph
N. The mayor's wife
O. Valinhos

The Children of Fatima   Mary Fabyan Windeatt

Chapters 6–10

Multiple Choice

Choose the correct response and circle the answer.

3 points each (30 points)

1. Which important man was infuriated when he found out about the children's visions?
   a. the pope
   b. the president
   c. the mayor
   d. the parish priest

2. Where did the Lady visit the children on August 19?
   a. the jail
   b. Valinhos
   c. the church
   d. the Cova

3. Who did the Lady say she was on October 13?
   a. an angel
   b. a devil
   c. the Lady of the Rosary
   d. St. Bernadette

4. What miracle did the crowds see on October 13?
   a. the sun dance
   b. the moon dance
   c. the world covered in water
   d. they all saw the Blessed Virgin

5. Where did the mayor take the children on August 13?
   a. the Cova
   b. the jail
   c. the ocean
   d. the church

6. What did the children do with the prisoners while in jail?
   a. said the Rosary with them
   b. hide from them
   c. ignore them
   d. play cards with them

7. Where did the mayor take the children after the jail?
   a. their home
   b. a convent
   c. the church
   d. his home

8. How did the crowd react to the miracle of the sun?
   a. they danced
   b. they sung
   c. they asked pardon for their sins
   d. they ran away

36 | *The Children of Fatima* Mary Fabyan Windeatt

Chapters 6–10
Quiz 2

9. How many people were at the Cova on August 13 while the children were in jail?

    a. 5,000
    b. 500
    c. 100,000
    d. 15,000

10. How many people were in attendance for the Lady's visit on October 13?

    a. 10
    b. 10,000
    c. 70,000
    d. 3,000

Narration Exercise

The remaining 12 points of the quiz will come from this narration exercise. Answer the question below in 2–5 complete sentences.

During the miracle of the dancing sun, the children experienced a new vision. What did they each see?

The Children of Fatima Mary Fabyan Windeatt

Chapter 11

The Victims

Key Terms

These are important people, places, and things you should remember from this chapter.

Maria de Carmo   The woman who had been cured from tuberculosis during the Lady's visit.

Maceira   A town twenty-two miles from Fatima, where Maria de Carmo journeyed from to be cured.

Tuberculosis   A disease that especially affects the lungs.

Vocabulary

*Read the sentences below and note the use of the word in **bold**. Write a definition or synonym for this word by considering its context.*

1. All Fatima was swept out of every appearance of **normalcy** by the miracle.

2. Truly, the **stupendous** wonder of October 13 had been well recorded by the cameras.

3. Atheistic Communism had been **unleashed** on Russia and the world.

4. The **mortifications** she had chosen were inclined to be extreme.

5. So the **penitential** side of their lives was kept secret.

The Victims — CHAPTER 11

Comprehension Questions

To better understand this chapter, ask yourself these questions and write down your answers using complete sentences.

1. How did Maria de Carmo make her pilgrimages to the Cova that led to her cure?

   ....
   ....
   ....

2. Which group was not convinced of the miracle at the Cova? How did they respond?

   ....
   ....
   ....

3. In what ways did Lucia's family change after the miracle took place? Did they treat her differently?

   ....
   ....
   ....

4. How did the children's lives change after the Lady's last visit?

   ....
   ....
   ....

5. What sacrifice did Lucia suggest the children do to suffer for souls?

   ....
   ....
   ....

The Children of Fatima Mary Fabyan Windeatt

CHAPTER 11: The Victims

Activity

The following is an optional activity meant to help you in your own prayer life.

Write down the prayer the children said when they were asking Our Lady to help them bear suffering. Discuss when this prayer could be useful in your life.

....
....
....
....
....
....
....
....
....
....
....
....
....
....
....
....
....
....
....
....

The Victims

CHAPTER 11

Color the picture of the three children giving away their lunches to those in need.

The Children of Fatima   Mary Fabyan Windeatt

CHAPTER 12

The Bells Toll in Fatima

Key Terms

These are important people, places, and things you should remember from this chapter.

Blessed Sacrament   The consecrated Host or Body and Blood of Jesus.

Tabernacle   A liturgical furnishing used to house the Eucharist outside of Mass.

Joyful Mysteries   Consist of the Annunciation, the Visitation, the Nativity, the Presentation, and the Finding of the Child Jesus in the Temple.

Sorrowful Mysteries   Consist of the Agony in the Garden, the Scourging at the Pillar, the Crowning with Thorns, the Carrying of the Cross, and the Crucifixion.

Glorious Mysteries   Consist of the Resurrection, the Ascension, the Descent of the Holy Spirit, the Assumption, and the Crowning of Mary as Queen of Heaven and Earth.

Vocabulary

*Read the sentences below and note the use of the word in **bold**. Write a definition or synonym for this word by considering its context.*

1. Both students and teachers were **consumed** with curiosity.

2. Soon she would take Jacinta and him to Heaven, leaving Lucia on earth for an **indefinite** period.

3. The funeral bells tolled in constant **requiem**.

4. Francisco was going to die very soon, but Jacinta—**convalescing** from the influenza and able to walk about—was going to suffer still more for souls.

The Bells Toll in Fatima

CHAPTER 12

Comprehension Questions

To better understand this chapter, ask yourself these questions and write down your answers using complete sentences.

1. Which of the children did not do so well in school? What happened as a result of this?

   ....
   ....
   ....

2. How did the children view the mysteries of the Rosary?

   ....
   ....
   ....

3. What came across Europe after the children had been going to school? Who was affected?

   ....
   ....
   ....

4. Why was Francisco convinced he would never recover?

   ....
   ....
   ....

5. What was Francisco permitted to do on his deathbed?

   ....
   ....
   ....

The Children of Fatima   Mary Fabyan Windeatt

CHAPTER 13: The Great Sacrifice

Key Terms

These are important people, places, and things you should remember from this chapter.

Pleurisy   A painful inflammation of the lining around the lungs.

St. Augustine's Hospital   A hospital in Ourem where Jacinta was moved to receive regular treatments.

Vocabulary

Read the sentences below and note the use of the word in **bold**. *Write a definition or synonym for this word by considering its context.*

1. A strange peace flooded the **grieving** mother's heart.

2. An **abscess** had formed in her side, and now there were many days when every breath was like a sharp sword thrust.

3. As always, there was real **conviction** in Jacinta's voice when she spoke of Hell.

4. Undoubtedly God's mercy was allowing the **merits** of Jacinta's heroic charity to be applied to sinners.

The Great Sacrifice

CHAPTER 13

Comprehension Questions

To better understand this chapter, ask yourself these questions and write down your answers using complete sentences.

1. What happened on April 4, 1919?

   ....
   ....
   ....

2. How did Jacinta's health change after her brother died?

   ....
   ....
   ....

3. What did Jacinta remind Lucia to do just before dying?

   ....
   ....
   ....

4. What was Jacinta granted permission to do while she was sick?

   ....
   ....
   ....

5. Where did Manuel and Olimpia send their sick daughter?

   ....
   ....
   ....

The Children of Fatima   Mary Fabyan Windeatt

CHAPTER 14 — To Lisbon

Key Terms

These are important people, places, and things you should remember from this chapter.

Orphanage of Our Lady of Miracles   The place Jacinta stayed before entering the hospital in Lisbon.

Sister Mary of the Purification   The director of the Orphanage of Our Lady of Miracles.

Doctor Leonardo de Castro Freire   One of the finest surgeons in Lisbon at the time who was to perform Jacinta's operation.

Vocabulary

*Read the sentences below and note the use of the word in **bold**. Write a definition or synonym for this word by considering its context.*

1. Slowly, surely the events **foretold** by the Blessed Mother on her latest visit were coming true.

2. They loved and **reverenced** her accordingly.

3. Naturally Sister Mary of the Purification was much impressed with the little newcomer's **piety**.

4. Then, **evading** the question, she began to speak in a faraway voice.

5. And as her godmother stared **incredulously,** she gave a little sigh.

The Children of Fatima   Mary Fabyan Windeatt

Chapter 14: To Lisbon

Comprehension Questions

To better understand this chapter, ask yourself these questions and write down your answers using complete sentences.

1. What news did Our Lady of the Rosary bring Jacinta when she visited her at home?

2. Where did Jacinta have to go before she could enter the hospital in Lisbon?

3. What visitor did Jacinta have frequently while staying at the orphanage?

4. What did the doctors do during Jacinta's surgery at St. Stephen's Hospital and what was the state of her health afterward?

5. What did Jacinta ask for ten days after surgery? Was this permitted?

CHAPTER 15: Farwell to Fatima

Key Terms

These are important people, places, and things you should remember from this chapter.

Baron d'Alvayazèr A devout nobleman who asked to keep Jacinta's mortal remains in his family vault at Ourem.

Jose Alves Correia da Silva The bishop of Leiria.

Sisters of St. Dorothy Boarding School The place Lucia was sent to school at fourteen by the bishop.

Maria das Dores The name Lucia went by when she went to boarding school.

Vocabulary

*Read the sentences below and note the use of the word in **bold**. Write a definition or synonym for this word by considering its context.*

1. Even the **consolation** of being able to pay frequent visits to Jacinta's grave was denied her.

2. Perhaps there might even be some **hysterical** women to claim that they had been cured of this or that ailment by the Blessed Virgin.

3. Her mother had **unwittingly** spoken as a prophetess when she said that this was Lucia's last day at home.

4. This earth, this dry and **porous** limestone, had belonged to her family for generations.

5. The Heart of Jesus wishes to be **venerated** together with the Immaculate Heart of His Mother.

48 | *The Children of Fatima* Mary Fabyan Windeatt

Farwell to Fatima

CHAPTER 15

Comprehension Questions

To better understand this chapter, ask yourself these questions and write down your answers using complete sentences.

1. Who asked a special favor of Jacinta's remains?

   ....
   ....
   ....

2. Why was Lucia's mother worried about her going to the Cova on May 13, 1920?

   ....
   ....
   ....

3. What did the Bishop of Leiria suggest to Lucia's mother?

   ....
   ....
   ....

4. What did the bishop want Lucia to change before she went to school?

   ....
   ....
   ....

5. Whose words did Lucia remember when she was praying in the chapel just before leaving home?

   ....
   ....
   ....

Quiz 3

Chapters 11–15

Name _____ Date _____ Score _____

Vocabulary

Complete the crossword puzzle using the definitions and synonyms below as clues. All answers will come from the vocabulary sections covered so far. Look back over these sections if you need assistance completing the puzzle. This should be the only part of the quiz where you can view your notes from previous sections.

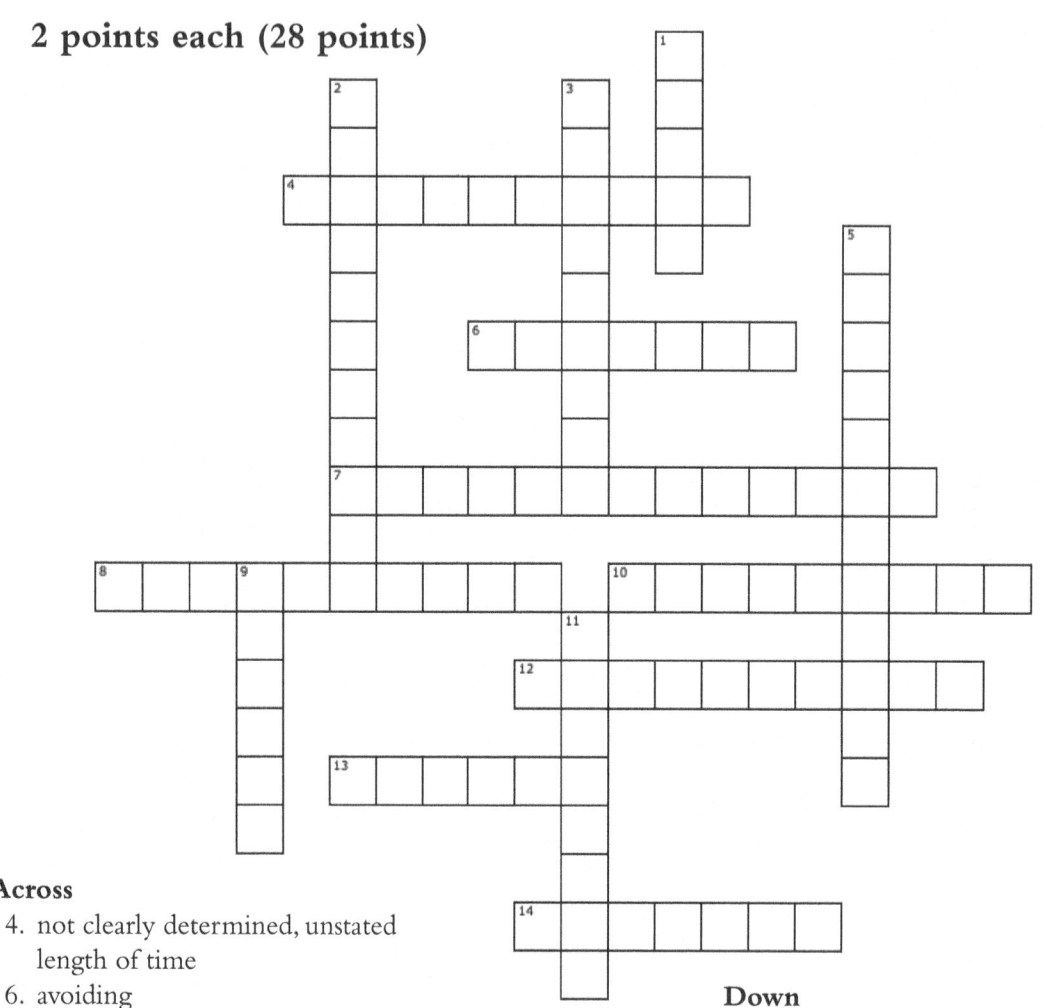

2 points each (28 points)

Across
4. not clearly determined, unstated length of time
6. avoiding
7. with disbelief
8. causing amazement
10. let loose
12. feeling of certainty; firmly held belief
13. claims to a spiritual reward
14. music or Church service for the dead

Down
1. devotion to God
2. something that gives cheer or lessens sorrow
3. honored
5. recovering one's health
9. having small spaces or holes for air or liquid to pass
11. engrossed with

The Children of Fatima Mary Fabyan Windeatt

Chapters 11–15

QUIZ 3

Key Terms

Match the correct term to its definition.

2 points each (28 points)

_____ A devout nobleman who asked to keep Jacinta's mortal remains in his family vault at Ourem.

_____ The bishop of Leiria.

_____ The place Lucia was sent to school at fourteen by the Bishop.

_____ The name Lucia went by when she went to boarding school.

_____ The place Jacinta stayed before entering the hospital in Lisbon.

_____ The director of the Orphanage of Our Lady of Miracles.

_____ One of the finest surgeons in Lisbon at the time who was to perform Jacinta's operation.

_____ A painful inflammation of the lining around the lungs.

_____ A hospital in Ourem where Jacinta was moved to receive regular treatments.

_____ The consecrated Host or Body or Blood of Jesus.

_____ A liturgical furnishing used to house the Eucharist outside of Mass.

_____ The woman who had been cured from tuberculosis during the Lady's visit.

_____ A town twenty-two miles from Fatima where Maria de Carmo journeyed from to be cured.

_____ A disease that especially affects the lungs.

A. Baron d'Alvayazèr
B. Blessed Sacrament
C. Doctor Leonardo de Castro Freire
D. Jose Alves Correia da Silva
E. Maceira
F. Maria das Dores
G. Maria de Carmo
H. Orphanage of Our Lady of Miracles
I. Pleurisy
J. St. Augustine's Hospital
K. Sister Mary of the Purification
L. Sisters of St. Dorothy Boarding School
M. Tabernacle
N. Tuberculosis

The Children of Fatima Mary Fabyan Windeatt

QUIZ 3 — Chapters 11–15

Multiple Choice

Choose the correct response and circle the answer.

3 points each (30 points)

1. What was Jacinta granted permission to do while she was sick?

    a. travel to Rome

    b. tend the sheep

    c. go to school

    d. receive communion

2. Where did the bishop of Leiria suggest Lucia go?

    a. to boarding school

    b. to Rome

    c. to America

    d. to a convent

3. Who frequently visited Jacinta when she was staying at the orphanage in Lisbon?

    a. Lucia

    b. Our Lady

    c. the doctor

    d. her mother

4. What did all three children do after the great miracle happened in October?

    a. started an orphanage

    b. moved away

    c. went to school

    d. became missionaries

5. Which child died first?

    a. Francisco

    b. Lucia

    c. Jacinta

6. What news did Our Lady bring Jacinta after she went home from the hospital in Ourem?

    a. she would be cured

    b. Lucia would die soon

    c. she would die alone

    d. all of the above

7. Who asked to keep Jacinta's remains?

    a. the pope

    b. Lucia

    c. Father Marques Ferriera

    d. Baron d'Alvayazèr

8. What happened in Europe that spread to Fatima?

    a. a great flood

    b. a plague

    c. a war

    d. a drought

The Children of Fatima Mary Fabyan Windeatt

Chapters 11–15

Quiz 3

9. What was Maria de Carmo cured of while at the Cova on October 13?

   a. tuberculosis
   b. cancer
   c. influenza
   d. arthritis

10. What material did the children tie around their waists as a sacrifice for sinners?

    a. string
    b. rope
    c. ribbon
    d. wire

Narration Exercise

The remaining 14 points of the quiz will come from this narration exercise. Answer the question below in 2–5 complete sentences.

What special visitor did Jacinta and Francisco have when they were infected with influenza? What did the visitor tell them?

The Children of Fatima Mary Fabyan Windeatt

Final Essay

Essay

To be written after completion of the novel and all quizzes. Graded at parent's discretion.

Explain what virtues the children of Fatima displayed that made them so holy. In what ways can you emulate them in your everyday life so that you too can practice these virtues?

Final Essay

Glossary

Aljustrel A town just outside of Fatima in Portugal.

Amelia A young girl who had died recently and would be in purgatory until the end of the world, according to the beautiful lady from heaven.

Angel of Peace The angel who appeared to the children and revealed his name as the Guardian Angel of Portugal.

Antonio dos Santos The father of Lucia.

Atheist A person who believes that God does not exist.

Baron d'Alvayazèr A devout nobleman who asked to keep Jacinta's mortal remains in his family vault at Ourem.

Blessed Sacrament The consecrated Host or Body and Blood of Jesus.

Communism A system of government in which a single party controls state-owned means of production with the aim of establishing a stateless society.

Cova da Iria A large hollow about a mile from the homes of the children in Fatima.

Doctor Leonardo de Castro Freire One of the finest surgeons in Lisbon at the time who was to perform Jacinta's operation.

Father Marques Ferreira A parish priest to the families of the children.

Fatima A village in Portugal where Jacinta, Francisco, and Lucia lived.

Feast of St. Anthony A great feast day celebrated by those in Portugal for the saint who had died in Padua but still belonged to Portugal.

First World War Took place from 1914 to 1918 and was happening during the Lady's visits to the children.

Five First Saturdays An Act of Reparation to the Immaculate Heart, where a person goes to Confession and receives communion on these days, as well as says the Rosary and spends fifteen minutes meditating on the mysteries of the Rosary.

Glossary

Francisco Brother to Jacinta and cousin to Lucia.

Glorious Mysteries Consist of the Resurrection, the Ascension, the Descent of the Holy Spirit, the Assumption, and the Crowning of Mary as Queen of Heaven and Earth.

Holy Family The Child Jesus with His mother, the Blessed Virgin, and foster father, Saint Joseph.

Immaculate Heart The Lady told them this was her heart; the heart of the Blessed Virgin.

Jacinta Sister to Francisco and cousin to Lucia.

Jose Alves Correia da Silva The bishop of Leiria.

Joyful Mysteries Consist of the Annunciation, the Visitation, the Nativity, the Presentation, and the Finding of the Child Jesus in the Temple.

Lady of Sorrows A name for the Blessed Virgin. She revealed herself to Lucia in this form on October 13.

Lisbon The capital of Portugal where Saint Anthony had been born.

Lucia Cousin to Jacinta and Francisco.

Maceira A town twenty-two miles from Fatima where Maria de Carmo journeyed from to be cured.

Manuel Marto The father of Jacinta and Francisco.

Maria das Dores The name Lucia went by when she went to boarding school.

Maria das Neves A young girl who had died recently and was in heaven, according to the beautiful lady from heaven.

Maria de Carmo The woman who had been cured from tuberculosis during the Lady's visit.

Maria Rosa dos Santos The mother of Lucia.

Glossary

Mayor of Ourem A man who tried to deviously stop the children from visiting Cova da Iria and force them to admit they were lying.

The mayor's wife A woman who was ashamed of her husband's actions and treated the children with care.

Newspaperman A man who tried to convince the people everything the children did was a trick for publicity.

Olimpia Marto The mother of Jacinta and Francisco.

Orphanage of Our Lady of Miracles The place Jacinta stayed before entering the hospital in Lisbon.

Our Lady of Mount Carmel A name for the Blessed Virgin. She revealed herself to Lucia in a brown habit holding the scapular of Mount Carmel.

Ourem The nearest town of any size to Fatima.

Pius XI Was to become a pope and reign from 1922 to 1939.

Pleurisy A painful inflammation of the lining around the lungs.

Porto-de-Mos A neighboring village to Fatima.

Russia The Lady told the children that Russia would be converted and would have peace if people followed her request.

St. Augustine's Hospital A hospital in Ourem where Jacinta was moved to receive regular treatments.

Saint Joseph The husband of Mary and foster father of Jesus who was to accompany the Lady to the Cova in October.

Sister Mary of the Purification The director of the Orphanage of Our Lady of Miracles.

Sisters of St. Dorothy Boarding School The place Lucia was sent to school at fourteen by the bishop.

Glossary

Sorrowful Mysteries Consist of the Agony in the Garden, the Scourging at the Pillar, the Crowning with Thorns, the Carrying of the Cross, and the Crucifixion.

Tabernacle A liturgical furnishing used to house the Eucharist outside of Mass.

Tuberculosis A disease that especially affects the lungs.

Valinhos A village some distance from the children's home.